DEAR BOSS,

By Pat Cooksey & Kevin Cullen

Pictures by Greg Allen

© Kevin Cullen and Pat Cooksey 2020

ISBN: 978-1-09831-642-6

eBook ISBN: 978-1-09831-643-3

Dear Boss, I write this note to you to tell you of my plight.
And at the time of writing, I am not a pretty sight ...

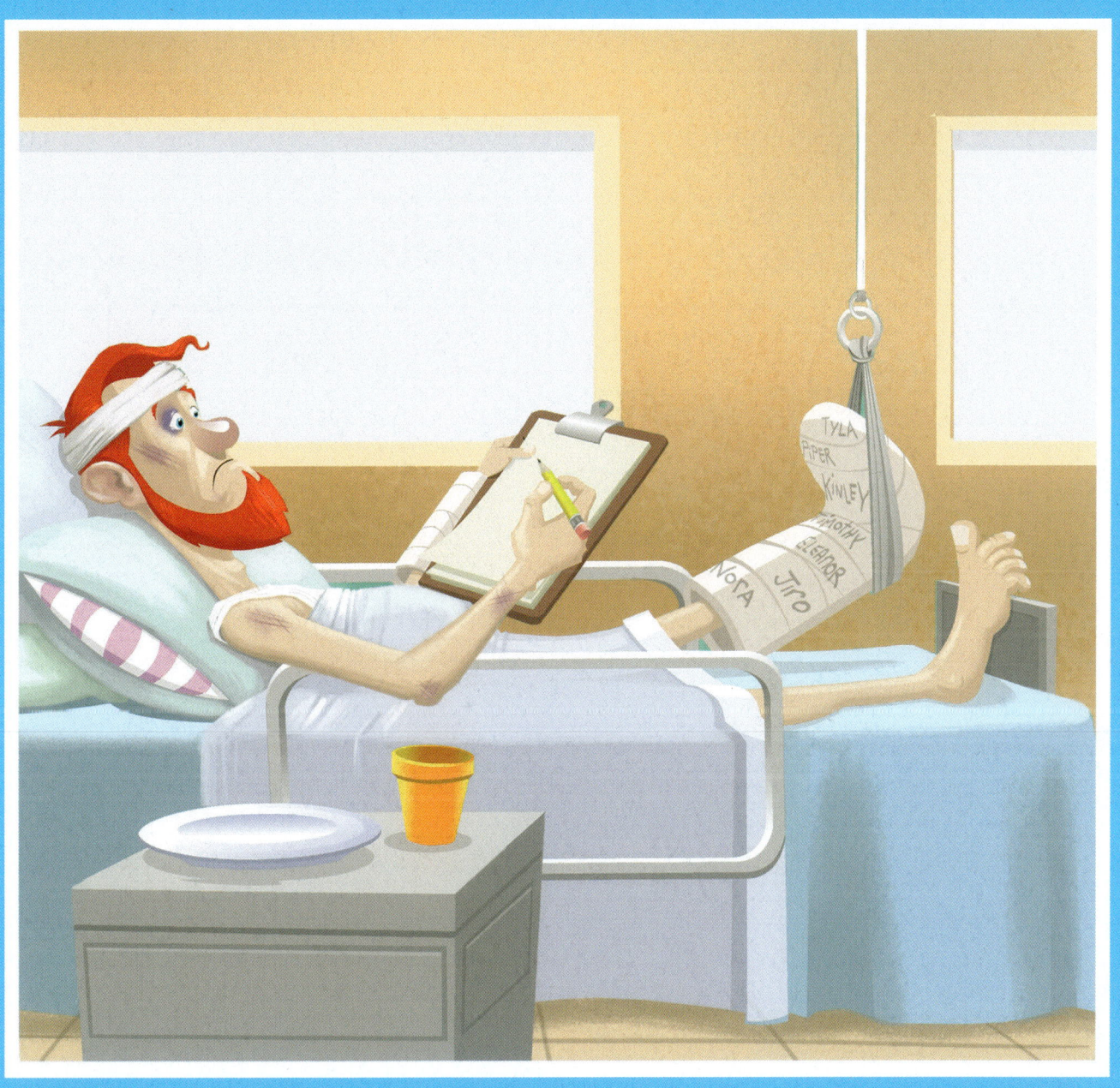

Me body is all black and blue, me face a deathly gray,
So I write this note to say why Paddy's not at work today.

While I was working on the 14th Floor,
some bricks I had to clear.
And to throw them down from such
a height, was not a good idea ...

The Foreman wasn't very pleased, he'd been an awful sod.
And he said I had to carry them down a latter in my hod.

Now shiftin' all these bricks by hand
to me seemed awful slow.

So I hoisted up a barrel and secured the rope below.

But in my haste to do the job, I was too blind to see ...

That a barrel full of building bricks
was heavier than me!

Now when I came down I cut the rope, and
the barrel fell like lead.

And clinging tightly to the rope, I started up instead ...
I shot up like a rocket, and to my dismay I found ...

That halfways up I met the bloody
barrel coming down!
Now the barrel it broke me
shoulder, as to the ground it sped ...

And when I reached the top, I struck the
pulley with me head!

Still holding on, though numbed in shock,
from this almighty blow ...

When the barrel spilled out half its
bricks, 14 floors below.

Now when the bricks had fallen
from the barrel to the floor ...

15

I then outweighed the barrel and I
started down once more ...

Still clinging tightly to the rope, I
headed for the ground ...

And landed all across the bricks that
were all scattered round!

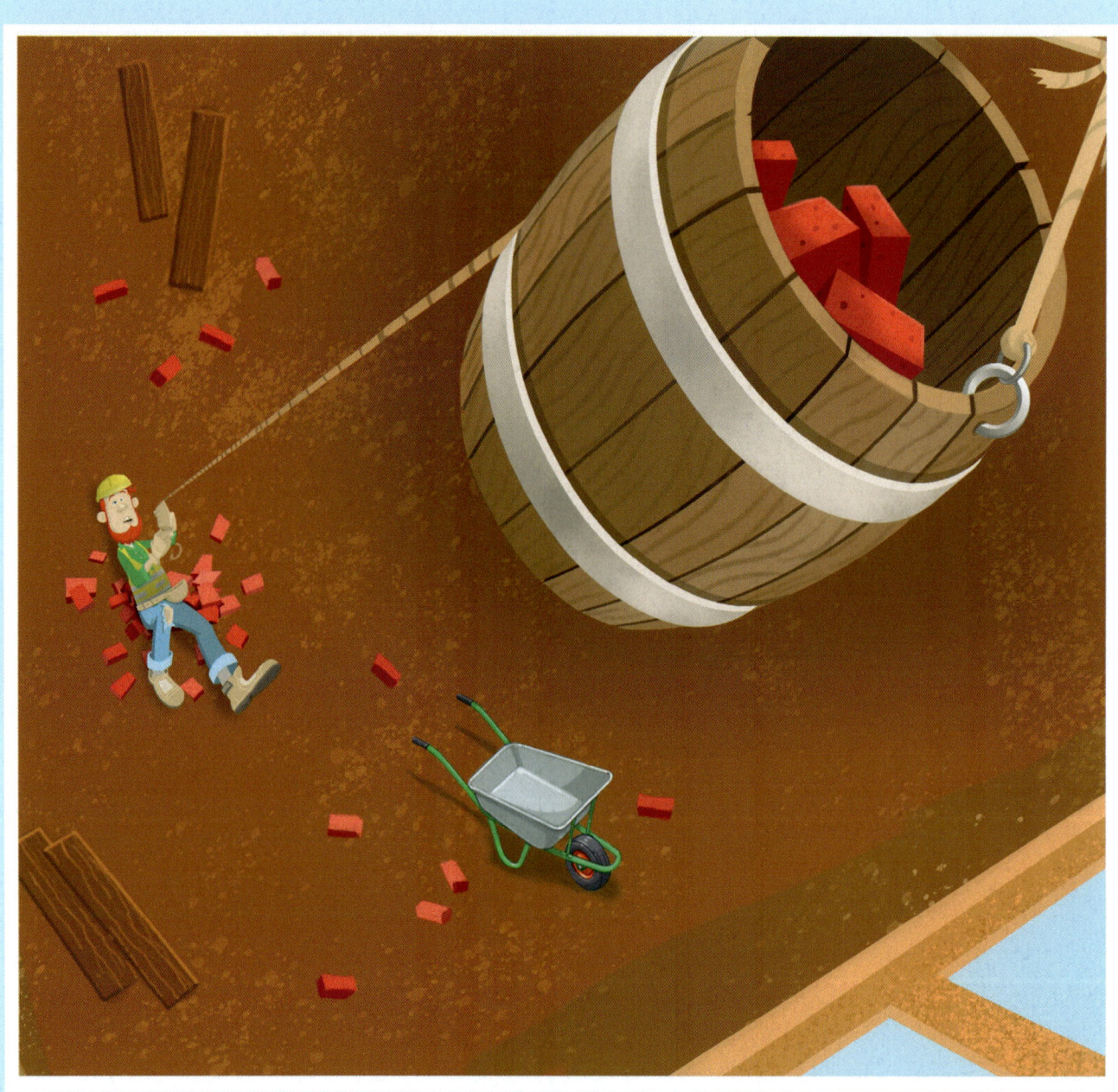

As I lay there moaning on the ground, I
thought I'd passed the worst ...

Then the barrel struck the pulley wheel
and didn't the bottom burst!

A shower of bricks came down on me,
I didn't have a hope.
And as I was losing consciousness, I let
go the bloody rope!

Now the barrel, it being heavier, it
started down once more ...

And landed right across me as I lay there on the floor ...

It broke three ribs and my left arm,
and I can only say ...

That I hope you'll understand why
Paddy's not at work today!